THE LION TAMER

A SHORT STORY
BY JOHN ALBERT BUCHNESS
1990

COVER PAINTING
BY CHARLOTTE LERCHE BUCHNESS

Copyright © 2023 John Albert Buchness.

All rights reserved. No part of this book may be reproduced, stored, or transmitted by any means—whether auditory, graphic, mechanical, or electronic—without written permission of both publisher and author, except in the case of brief excerpts used in critical articles and reviews. Unauthorized reproduction of any part of this work is illegal and is punishable by law.

ISBN: 979-8-89031-794-0 (sc)
ISBN: 979-8-89031-795-7 (hc)
ISBN: 979-8-89031-516-8 (e)

Because of the dynamic nature of the Internet, any web addresses or links contained in this book may have changed since publication and may no longer be valid. The views expressed in this work are solely those of the author and do not necessarily reflect the views of the publisher, and the publisher hereby disclaims any responsibility for them.

One Galleria Blvd., Suite 1900, Metairie, LA 70001
(504) 702-6708

THE ILLUSTRATOR, CHARLOTTE LERCHE BUCHNESS, HOLDS A DISTINGUISHED DEGREE FROM THE DANISH ROYAL ACADEMY IN ARCHITECTURE, A TESTAMENT TO HER EXCEPTIONAL ARTISTIC PROWESS. IN A SERENDIPITOUS TWIST, SHE ALSO PROUDLY CARRIES DUAL CITIZENSHIP IN THE UNITED STATES, A COUNTRY SHE CALLS HOME ALONGSIDE HER HUSBAND, JOHN, WHO HAPPENS TO BE THE AUTHOR OF THE WORK.

PREFACE

THIS IS A STORY ON MANY LEVELS, BUT MAINLY OF THE LEVEL OF THE CHILD'S HEART, AND THEREFORE, ON THE LEVEL OF THE HEART OF HEARTS, AS THE CHILD'S HEART CONTAINS THE INFINITE WISDOM OF ALL THE SAGES, AND OF ALL THE AGES. THIS STORY IS ADDRESSED TO THE CHILD'S HEART IN EVERY MAN, SOMETIMES TO REBUKE, AND ALSO TO ASK HIM TO SHIFT THE SHAPE OF HIS SOUL TO ONE OF THE CREATURES HE SUPPOSEDLY HAS DOMINION OVER ON THIS PLANET.

IT IS TEARFULLY, AND DEVOTEDLY DEDICATED TO MY SPIRITUAL TEACHER AND MASTER, THE GURU, SRI CHINMOY, AND TO THE LION OF JUDAH, THE GREATEST JEW, MUSLIM, HINDU, CATHOLIC, PROTESTANT, AND BUDDHIST, THE CHRIST, JESUS.

THIS IS NOT A STORY OF RELIGION, OR ADVOCATING VEGETARIANISM, BUT EXPERIENCE PROVES THE HIGHER VISION IS AVAILABLE ONLY TO THOSE WHO NO LONGER KILL FOR THEIR FOOD.

THIS STORY IS WRITTEN FOR AIMEÉ, AND DANIEL BUCHNESS, MY CHILDREN, TO WHOM IT IS ALSO DEDICATED, IN HOPES THAT AS THEY GROW, THEY CAN SEE MY TRUTH, AND GREAT LOVE FOR THEM, DESPITE THE ZOO KEEPERS OF OUR WORLD, AND OF COURSE, THE P. T. BARNUMS.

FINALLY, THIS IS A STORY OF HUMAN PERSECUTION OF ARTISTS, AND MORE

IMPORTANTLY, OF COURAGE, IN THE FACE OF DOUBT, JEALOUSY, FEAR, AND RESTLESSNESS.

I WISH TO LEAVE WITH A QUOTE FROM THE BHAGAVAD GITA, INDIA'S WONDERFUL BOOK OF LIGHT: FOR ONE WHO HAS CONQUERED THE MIND, THE SUPER SOUL (GOD) IS ALREADY REACHED AND TRANQUILITY ATTAINED. TO SUCH A MAN, HAPPINESS AND DISTRESS, HEAT AND COLD, HONOR AND DISHONOR, ARE ALL THE SAME."

CREDITS

SALUTATIONS TO THE 26 WICOMICO COUNTY HIGH SCHOOL STUDENTS FROM MS. PRINGLE'S CLASS WHO CONTRIBUTED SCENES FOR THE CHAPTER, "THE ZOO PURCHASE, AND ESPECIALLY TO CRYSTAL HITCHCOCK, HOPE ORNDOFFT CHAD SWANSON, RYAN WALLING, KRISTIN BAKER, AND OF COURSE, TO THE YOUNG LADY WHO IDENTIFIED HERSELF SIMPLY, AS "JANE DOE."

CHAPTER 1

THE GREAT GRANDFATHER LION

THE LION TAMER

ONCE UPON A TIME, THERE WAS A ZOO. THE LIONS AND THE TIGERS LIVED SORT OF HAPPILY BECAUSE ALMOST EVERY DAY. THEIR KEEPER BROUGHT THEM MEAT THAT WAS TORN FROM THE SKELETONS OF THEIR KILLED BROTHERS AND SISTERS, THE OTHER FOUR-FOOTED ANIMALS. ANYWAY, THEY FELT SAFE.

ON THE LEFT SIDE OF THEIR BIG CAGE LIVED THE MONKEYS, OF ALL KINDS. TO THE RIGHT

LIVED THE APES, BIG, AND BULKY SLOW TAKING GOOD CARE OF THEIR YOUNG.

THE ZOO KEEPER, WHO BROUGHT THE FLESH NEARLY EVERY DAY HAD A FAVORITE: MAMA LION. SHE USED TO SHAG HER HAIR IN FRONT, AND TO THE SIDES OF HER HEAD, LIKE MAMA LIONS DO.

DON, THE KEEPER, WAS DEVOTED TO THESE FOUR-PAWED CREATURES. HE ALWAYS BROUGHT THEIR FOOD, EXCEPT ON THE DAYS AFTER HE DRANK BEER, OR WHATEVER DRINK SUITED HIS FANCY AT NIGHT. ALTHOUGH HE ALWAYS FED THEM ON THE DAYS HE DRANK, SOMETIMES FOR TWO DAYS AFTER HE'D NEGLECT THEM ALTOGETHER. FOR THE KIDS THESE DAYS WERE MISERABLE.

FOR THE GROWN LIONS AND TIGERS IT WAS A CHANCE TO THINK AND MEDITATE WITH THEIR EYES HALF CLOSED LIKE THEY DO, SOMETIMES GAZING ON' THE SUNSHINE. THE KIDS WOULD

RUN AND JUMP, FOR A WHILE UNTIL THEY SOON BECAME EXHAUSTED.

DURING THESE DAYS MAMA LION WOULD BE TERRIBLE: LIKE ANIMALS DO, SHE WOULD TERRORIZE THE KIDS INTO STAYING OUT OF TROUBLE, AND GOING TO BED ON TIME. ALL IN ALL, A LITTLE BORING, THEY ENJOYED A GOOD LIFE IN THE BIG CAGE, MAMA LION MAKING DISPLAYS OF AFFECTION NOW AND THEN, LICKING THE KIDS CLEAN, TEASING THEIR NECKS, AND MAKING SOFT GROWLS OF PRIDE TO DON, TO GET HIM TO TOSS THE MEAT NEARER HER DIRECTION. BEING SLIGHTLY ROTTED IT WAS EASIER FOR THE KIDS TO DIGEST. THE GROWN JUST ATE LESS, AS IT IS THE ANIMAL NATURE TO ENJOY A FRESH KILL. UNABLE TO KILL FOR THEMSELVES, LIKE BACK HOME, THE GROWN FELT COMFORTABLE WITH THE FRESH ARMS, LEGS, AND HEARTS OF THE OTHER LESS FORTUNATE CREATURES.

SOMETIME AFTER EATING THE GROWN LIONS AND TIGERS WOULD FALL OFF TO SLEEP,

WHILE THE KIDS WOULD BECOME QUIETED BF THE STRANGE SENSATIONS OF DIGESTION, AND HOW THE SUNLIGHT SEEMED TO BEAT ON THEIR EYELIDS AT THOSE TIMES!

THE "GREAT GRANDFATHER LION," NOW LONG GONE, USED TO SPEAK ON SLEEP AS A LION'S MEDITATION ON "NOTHINGNESS". AFTER FEEDING, SOME OF THE OLDER BOYS WOULD REMARK, QUESTIONINGLY, "THE GROWN SURE SLEEP A LOT." WHEN HE'D BRING THE MEAT, DON HAD A LITTLE LAUGH, ACTUALLY, A YUK, AND THE OLDER BOYS WONDERED ABOUT IT. THEY WOULD PRACTICE THEIR ROARS, AT TIMES TOGETHER, AND ONCE DURING THE BOYS' DISPLAY OF A LION'S CHARACTER THIS WAY, DON'S HELPER ASKED HIM WHY HE LAUGHED THAT WAY. HE JUST SAID, "I LIKE IT THAT WAY. THE BOYS, NOTICING THIS, WONDERED WHY THE OTHER HUMAN, DON'S HELPER, DIDN'T ALSO LAUGH LIKE THE MONKEYS NEXT DOOR. YOU SEE, YOUNG LIONS CAN NOT YET TELL THE DIFFERENCE BETWEEN HUMANS AND

MONKEYS, THOUGH THEY SEE CLEARLY THAT THE LARGE APES ON THE OTHER SIDE OF THEIR CAGE, ARE NOT AT ALL LIKE EITHER MONKEYS OR HUMANS.

AT TIMES THE YOUNG BOY LIONS WOULD DISCUSS THEIR FEAR OF THE LARGE APES: "YOU KNOW, THEY ARE SO GENTLE WITH THEIR KIDS WHEN I ROAR SOMETIMES TOO LOUDLY A FATHER WILL DO ONE OF THOSE DEEP HUMS FROM THE CENTER OF HIS BIG CHEST VIBRATE RIGHT THROUGH MY EARS, AND NECK. I'D HATE TO GET ONE OF THEM MAD AT ME," SAID YOUNG TACO LION.

"YES, THEY'RE SCARY," SAID YOUNG TANNY LION, "BUT THEY ARE SURE A LOT MORE PATIENT WITH THEIR KIDS THAN MAMA LION IS WITH US.

"YOU'RE RIGHT, PURRED A LITTLE GIRL CUB, WHO OVERHEARD THE BOYS, WHO WAS CALLED EMMY."

THE OLDER TIGERS REMEMBERED BACK IN BENGAL, IN INDIA; REMEMBER THE TALL SOFT GRASSES THEY WOULD MUNCH ON, THE SMALL BERRIES AND OTHER FRUITS THAT WOULD FIRE THEIR MUSCLES, MAKING THEM FAST, AND DECISIVE. THOSE WERE THE TIMES, THEY THOUGHT, REALLY ALIVE IN THEIR SHORT HAIR OF GOLD, ORANGE, BLACK AND WHITE, THE LIONS RESPECTED SO MUCH. THE BENGALS LOVED THE LION FAMILY BUT AVOIDED THE FATTY POUCHES, AND DOUBLE CHINS THE LIONS GET FROM OVERINDULGING EVERY DAY.

FRIENDS WITH THE LIONS FOR THOUSANDS OF YEARS THE BEAUTIFUL BENGALS WERE BETTER JUMPERS THAN THE LIONS, AND PRACTICED EACH DAY, EVEN THE OLDEST AMONG THEM, JUMPING UP THE BARS AND BRANCHES PROVIDED BY THE ZOO. THE MONKEYS TO THEIR RIGHT WOULD STUDY THEIR LIGHTNESS, IMITATING THE WAY MONKEYS DO, WITHOUT KNOWING WHY. TRYING TO ADOPT THE BENGAL MOVEMENTS THEY COULD ONLY

SWING AND HANG, SHOUTING TO ONE ANOTHER TO WATCH, IN VOICES LIKE SHRIEKS. TRY AS THEY MAY, WASTING PART OF THEIR ENERGY ON THE CRIES, THEY COULD NOT TURN IN MID-AIR LIKE THE TIGERS.

ABLE TO LIGHTEN HIS OWN BODY THE BENGAL COULD MOVE IN A CIRCLE, EVEN IN THE AIR, WHILE FLYING. MASTERS OF EVEN THE SMALLEST MOVEMENTS, WERE REVERED BY ALL THE OTHER ZOO CREATURES. STORIES WERE TOLD BY THE OLDER ONES ABOUT HOW THEY CAPTURED BIRDS IN-FLIGHT, ONLY TO LET THEM GO, ONLY TO CHALLENGE THEIR SPIRIT AND ABILITIES.

QUIET AND SHY, THEY SMILED AT THE LIONS' SOMETIMES ROARING CONTESTS, ESPECIALLY BETWEEN MAMA LION AND THE OTHERS. BUT THIS MADE THE TIGER MAMAS BLUSH, DISTRACTING THEM FROM THEIR THOUGHTS ABOUT THE LIONS' LONG WONDERFUL GOLDEN HAIR.

WATCHING THE LIONS PREENING FOR HOURS GAVE THEM GREAT JOY, IN AND OF ITSELF, WITHOUT THEIR CRAVING FOR LONG HAIR, WITHOUT ANY FEELINGS OF JEALOUSY. THE MONKEY FEMALES WOULD WATCH THE TIGERS IN IMITATION LIKE MONKEYS DO, AND WITH DIFFERENT ATTITUDES, THE LION TAMER MADE JERKING, COMBING MOTIONS ON ONE ANOTHER FOR THE TIGERS' ATTENTION. THIS ALSO MADE THE TIGER MAMAS BLUSH.

AT TIMES, DON, THOUGHT HE WAS GETTING THE TIGER MAMAS TO PERFORM THEIR FEATS FOR HIM, TRIED TO TRICK THEM, WITHHOLDING LEAN PIECES, WHILE THE WISE TIGER MAMAS WOULD SIGNAL TO ONE ANOTHER, WITHOUT HIS NOTICE, THEIR NEXT MOVES. FINELY COORDINATED THEY CREATED A PERFECT ILLUSION TO PLEASE HIM. AT OTHER TIMES, THINKING TO DISTRACT THE TIGERS, HE WOULD SWING HIS HEAVY CHAIN AGAINST THE CAGE WHILE THEY LOOKED AWAY • CRACK-DRANG! THE METAL VIBRATED IN A LOW AND MEAN VIBRATION.

THINKING TO CATCH THE BEAUTIFUL CREATURES OFF GUARD, AS HUMANS DO, HE WOULD LAUGH UNDER HIS BREATH, AND THINK TO HIMSELF, ALWAYS KEEP 'THEM GUESSING."

DON, THE ZOOKEEPER

CHAPTER 2

THE GREAT ONE, THE MOTHER LION

"BUT DADDY LION SAYS WE PRETEND UNTIL WE MAKE IT REAL".

AS ONLOOKERS, BROTHER TANNY, TACO, AND VINCENT, LAUGHED AT EMMY'S ATTEMPT TO STALK WHAT LITTLE GRASS GREW IN THEIR LARGE CAGE, NEAR THE REAR.

"WHAT'S YA HUNT IN', EMMY, YOUNG TANIOY LION INQUIRED, GENTLY, AS ALWAYS, (AND ALWAYS WITH A CHUCKLE)".

WITH HER USUAL ENTHUSIASM AND HER CHIPPED FRONT TOOTH, EMMY REPLIED HURRIEDLY:

"GREAT GRANDFATHER LION SAID SOME DADDY LIONS ROAMING FREE WITHOUT A MATE WILL EVEN KILL US" SHE SAID.

COUNTERED TANNY: "NO, EMMY, HE WAS TALKING ABOUT THOSE DADDY LIONS THAT THE PRIDE LETS PRACTISE THE 'LAW' OF THE JUNGLE. 'LAWYER' LIONS ALWAYS KILL THE YOUNG WHEN THEY'RE RUNNING FREE THROUGH THE TALL GRASSES. WHEN YOU GO OUT ONTO THE PLAIN, WHEN YOU'RE BIG, YOU'RE SUPPOSED TO WATCH OUT FOR THEM MOST OF ALL THEY WANT TO CONTROL EVERYTHING BUT THEMSELVES," HE CONCLUDED SADLY, AFTER A PAUSE.

UNDAUNTED, EMMY CONTINUED: "WELL, THE GREAT ONE", THE MOTHER OF ALL THE LIONS AND TIGERS, SAID SHE WATCHED AND STUDIED

THE LONE WOLF AND THE RATTLESNAKE, WHILE SHE WATCHED HER CUBS.

"DID SHE THINK THEY'D COME AFTER HER CUBS!?" INTERRUPTED TANNY.

"NOOO! TANNY, YOU'RE ALWAYS INTERUPTIN'. SHE SAID THEY WERE GOOD, AS GOOD AS LIONS, AND THEY WERE SMART, TOO, GOOD HUNTERS, ALWAYS HAVE ALL THE ESCAPES FIGURED OUT." ESCAPES FIGURED OUT?" - TANNY. LITTLE EMMY FELT PROUD: YEAH, THEY KNOW' D BEFORE THEY NEEDED TO HOW TO MOVE OR ESCAPE. THEY'RE BEAUTIFUL ANIMALS, SHE CONCLUDED WITH A TUG ON THE FIRST PART OF THE WORD BEAUTIFUL. TACO, A LITTLE CONFUSED, ASKED IF THE RATTLESNAKE DIDN'T ATTACK THE PRIDE. BOLTING UP AT HER CHEST, LITTLE EMMY LION QUICKLY RESPONDED THAT THE RATTLESNAKE ALWAYS MOVED SLOWLY TO ESCAPE, SOMETIMES SLOWLY EVEN WHEN CORNERED, LIKE WHEN CORNERED BY HUMANS T AND ONLY COUNTER-ATTACKED, SWIFTLY.

"MOST LIONS ARE HUMANS," SAID TANNY SARCASTICALLY, ONCE AGAIN INTERRUPTING HIS LITTLE SISTER, FOR HER ATTENTION.

"TANNY, YOU'RE ALWAYS SAYING NASTY THINGS, COUNTERED EMMY "THEY ARE NOT, LIONS ARE NICE SHE ADDED, SEEMING ALMOST NOT TO NOTICE TANNY'S IRRELEVANT INTERRUPTION, BUT ANOTHER CHANCE TO GIVE HIM INSTRUCTION.

"AND WHAT DID THE GREAT ONE SAY ABOUT THE WOLVES? DOESN'T THE LONE WOLF ATTACK THE BABY WILDEBEAST, IN A PACK?" ASKED VINCENT, STEPPING OUT OF HIS USUAL NEAR-TOTAL SILENCE.

DISTRACTED BY FEEDING TIME, THE YOUNG LIONS WATCHED THEIR KEEPER'S APPROACH. STARING INTENTLY AT VINCENT, THE KEEPER, DON, THREW A LEAN LIMB DIRECTLY AT HIM, SO HE HAD TO DODGE IT.

VINCENT'S EYESIGHT WAS REMARKABLE AMONG THE YOUNG LIONS, AS THOUGH HE HAD TWO PAIRS OF EYES, ONE PAIR FOR FRONT VISION, AND ONE PAIR FOR THE SIDE AND THE BACK. OF ALL THE LIONS, HIS STUDY OF THE CREATURES AROUND HIM, ESPECIALLY OF THE BENGALS, GAVE HIM A HIGH JUMP LIKE NO OTHER, DON USUALLY ANTAGONIZED VINCENT FIRST, SAYING "LET'S SEE YA JUMP FROM THIS ONE, BABE!"

VINCENT LION QUIETLY ENDURED THIS HARASSMENT, NOT KNOWING HOW SHORTLY THIS TRAINING WOULD BE INVALUABLE TO HIM.

"THE GREAT ONE, MOTHER LION, MANY GENERATIONS AGO, TRAVERSED THE EARTH IN MANY ENVIRONMENTS. THIS WAS BEFORE THE OCEAN COVERED THE MAJOR PART OF THE EARTH'S SURFACE. WITH MANY REARINGS OF LION CUBS, SHE OBSERVED THE EARTH'S CREATURES WITH A CURIOUS DETACHMENT.

HER STORYTELLING IS RECORDED IN LION HISTORY.

"OF ALL THE CREATURES OF THIS EARTH," SHE SAID, "THE EAGLE—BIRD, AND THE WOLF, ARE THE MOST NOBLE, TAKING ONLY ONE MATE FOR LIFE. OF ALL THE CREATURES, THE LION, TIGER, AND DEER, ARE THE MOST COURAGEOUS.

QUIETLY, THE WOLF AND THE EAGLE PAIR REMAIN TOGETHER ALL ITS LIFE, NURSING ONE ANOTHER'S INJURIES, AND NURSING TOGETHER YOUNG. OF ALL THE FATHERS THE WOLF FATHER IS THE BEST AND TAKES CARE OF THE CUBS RIGHT FROM BIRTH, LEAVING THE MOTHER WOLF TO REST, AND RECOVER FROM THE LITTER. HE TEACHES THE CUBS, AND HE FEEDS THEM AS SOON AS THE MOTHER CAN STOP NURSING EVEN IF SHE IS TIRED, HE WILL CHEW FOR THE CUBS TO ENSURE THEIR SURVIVAL. THE EAGLE PARENTS BOTH WILL DO THIS ALSO. THE HIGHEST-FLYING WINGED CREATURES, WILL TEACH THEIR YOUNG TO FLY AS SOON AS POSSIBLE.

THE WOLF PACK HAS A MALE, CALLED THE 'LONE WOLF' A MYSTERY IN THEIR CLOSE FAMILY ORGANIZATION. HE ALONE LEAVES THE PACK, AND NO ONE KNOWS WHY. AS A YOUNG ADULT, HE WILL LEAVE THE HOME FOR MORE NORTHERN TERRITORY, YET NEVER WILL HE CLAIM TERRITORY, AS WOLVES ARE NORMALLY THOUGHT TO DO, BY HUMANS. IT IS AS IF HE MUST SEE THE ENTIRE CREATION, OR AS MUCH OF IT AS HIS POWERFUL LEGS WILL CARRY HIM TO. IN THE DAYS OF THE EARLIEST LIONS, HE AND THE WOLF FAMILY EXISTED TOGETHER ON THE EARTH, AS WOLF FAMILY LONE WOLF.

THE LONE WOLF ONLY BANDS WITH A PACK, AS ALL WOLVES DO, WHEN THREATENED BY STARVATION, AND AT THAT TIME THEY WILL COORDINATE TO TAKE DOWN PREY. IN THEIR USUAL HYPOCRISY THE HUMAN CREATURES AT ONCE FEAR THE WOLF, AND CALL HIM THEIR BEST FRIEND. THEY IGNORANTLY BELIEVE THAT A WOLF WILL ATTACK THEM INSTINCTIVELY. YET, WOLVES, ESPECIALLY THE LONE WOLF, WILL AVOID THE HUMAN CREATURE

WHENEVER POSSIBLE, REALIZING THAT AN ANIMAL WITHOUT PURITY CAN KNOW NO REAL COURAGE, AND THEREFORE CANNOT KNOW HIS TRUE DESIRES FOR LIFE. AND THE LONE WOLF, THOUGH A MYSTERY, KNOWS THE IMPORTANCE OF FREEDOM AND COURAGE.

HE IS CAUTIOUS, FIRST, REALIZING THAT ANOTHER CREATURE UNSURE OF HIMSELF, IS HIS MOST DANGEROUS ENEMY. THE BUCK DEER, THE FATHER, IS THE FASTEST, AND THE STRONGEST. HE KNOWS THIS AND THEREFORE KNOWS HIS PLACE. IF ANY ARE TO BE SACRIFICED TO DANGER, IT MUST BE HE. HE LEADS THE DOE AND THE FAUN BY TEN LION LEAPS AHEAD, WHILE THEY WATCH HIS HEAD MOVEMENTS FOR SIGNALS OF THE NEXT DIRECTION TO FLY. THEIRS IS MORE LIKE FLIGHT THAN A LEAP.

CROSSING A HUMAN TRAIL, THE BUCK LEAVES BEHIND A SCENT OF COME FORWARD OR STAY BEHIND, TO THE DOE. HE ADVANCES WITH COMPLETE SELF—SACRIFICE AND

WITH COMPLETE COURAGE, TO LEAD THE WAY OUT OF THE FOREST. WITH HIS ACT OF COURAGE AND DOE AND FAUN DUPLICATE HIS FLIGHT" YOUNG TACO LION WEIGHED THE PROBLEM OF THE LONE WOLF IN THE PACK AND BABY WILDEBEAST. WHAT IF HE TAKES A FEMALE?

HE WONDERED. WILL HE LATER VIOLATE THE WOLF CODE AND LEAVE HER? THEN PONDERING THE FACE, HE HAS NEVER HEARD OF A LONE-MOTHER WOLF HE REALIZED THAT MATING IS THE ONLY EVENT IN THE LONE WOLF'S LIFE THAT COULD CHANGE HIS NORMAL HERMIT LIFE. SATISFIED, HE ANSWERED FINALLY, VINCENT'S QUERY: "THE LONE WOLVES FORM A PACK ONLY TO END STARVATION, LIKE IN A DROUGHT OR A BLIZZARD!

DOE AND FAUN

CHAPTER 3

THE ZOO PURCHASE: DAMIAN, THE LION TAMER

HAS NOT THE LORD MADE THEM ONE? BECAUSE HE WAS SEEKING GODLY OFFSPRING. SO, GUARD YOURSELF IN YOUR SPIRIT, AND DO NOT BREAK FAITH WITH THE WIFE OF YOUR YOUTH.

"I HATE DIVORCE, SAYS THE LORD GOD OF ISRAEL, AND L HATE A MAN'S COVERING HIMSELF WITH VIOLENCE AS WELL AS WITH HIS GARMENTS," SAYS THE LORD ALMIGHTY. SO, GUARD YOURSELF IN SPIRIT AND DO NOT BREAK YOUR FAITH

"HE WILL TURN THE HEARTS OF THE FATHERS TO THEIR CHILDREN, AND THE HEARTS OF THE CHILDREN TO THEIR FATHERS, OR ELSE I WILL COME AND STRIKE THE LAND WITH A CURSE." - THE BOOK OF MALACHI CHAPTER 4 OF THE OLD TESTAMENT

"HEY, WHAT'S THOSE BLUE LIGHTS, TANNY, AND DO YOU HEAR THOSE DOGS BARKING OVER THERE?

"LITTLE EMMY CUB ASKED, AS HER SMALL FRAME POINTED STIFFLY IN THE DIRECTION OF THE ZOOKEEPER'S APARTMENT WINDOW.

NEARING DUSK IN MAY, A WARM SPRING EVENING, THE SLOWLY MOVING TRAIN CAME TO AN UNSTARTLING HALT. ALL WAS QUIET IN THE SMALL TOWN OF TIMESVILLE. THE RUSTY, SENILE TRAIN HAD P. T. BARNUM CIRCUS IN BRIGHT RED COLORS ON EACH CAR, IT WAS RUMORED THAT THE CIRCUS WAS COMING TO REMOTE TIMESVILLE, YET MOST DOUBTED IT WOULD EVER REALLY HAPPEN.

"I SMELL SOMEONE BURNING OVER THERE" TANNY JOLTED IN RESPONSE TO EMMY, "IS ANYONE MISSING?"

"DO WOLVES ROAST THEIR FOOD?" ASKED YOUNG VINCENT LION.

"I DON'T THINK SO," SAID TACO LION

"SOMETIMES I'VE HEARD OF THEM STEALING FROM CAMPS OF HUMANS AFTER THEY BURN SOMEONE"

"THEN, I GUESS WHEN HUNTING WITH WOLVES ITS BETTER TO BE A FOX", SAID VINCENT LION, IN HIS USUAL DIMENSION OF CLEVERNESS.

MAMA LION WALKED OVER AND SAID: "THAT'S DON COOKING A LAMB, EMMY"

"WHAT'S A LAMB, MAMA?" FATHER LION, NEARBY EXAMINING THE DENSITY IN THE ATMOSPHERE OF THE REMAINING SUNLIGHT,

CARESSED THE TOP OF EMMY'S SHOULDER WITH HIS POWERFUL JAW:

"THAT IS ONE OF THE SHEEP FAMILY, EM. THAT'S ONE OF THE ONLY ANIMALS I'VE EVER OBSERVED THAT WHEN IT'S NOT FEELING WELL, LAYS DOWN, AND WISHES TO DIE" HE GAVE A PONDEROUS FACE AND LOOKED UPWARDS AGAIN TOWARD THE EVENING SKY.

"WOW," SAID TANNY AND VINCENT, ALMOST IN UNISON.

"WHY WOULD AN ANIMAL WANT TO DO THAT? ASKED TACO.

"DON'T KNOW", SAID FATHER, AND MOVED OFF TOWARD THE REAR OF THE PRIDES' CAGE FOR HIS EVENING MEDITATION.

FATHER LION WAS A TEACHER IN THE PRIDE AND HAD A PROFOUND UNDERSTANDING OF LION LAW AND LION CHEMISTRY. HE HAD ATTENDED LECTURES ON LIONS' GENETICS

AND LIONS' CHEMISTRY WITH THE GREAT LION CHEMIST, LINUS PAWLING, AND THE GREAT LION PROFESSOR OF LAW AND ETHICS, THE REX AIKEN. THE REX AIKEN HAD BEFRIENDED FATHER LION, WHILE HE STUDIED AT THE UNIVERSITY ON THE WEST COAST OF AFRICA, BEFORE HIS CAPTURE BY THE HUMANS. IT WAS IN THE LION COMMUNITY KNOWN AS ZAIREKELY, A PLACE INHABITED BY HUMBLE LIONS WITH SINCERE DESIRES TO LEARN ALL THEY COULD OF THE LION'S NATURE.

IN THE REMOTE REGIONS OF CENTRAL AFRICA IT WAS DESCRIBED. AS A VILLAGE OF MYSTERY AND WAS GREATLY RESPECTED. AROUND THE EAST COAST OF AFRICA IT WAS CONSIDERED CONTENTIOUS, AND IRRELEVANT, BY THE JEALOUS LION COMMUNITIES LIVING THERE.

WHILE AT ZAIREKELY FATHER LION HAD WORKED AS A RESEARCHER AND WRITER TO ELECT A NEW LION KING FOR THE CONTINENT, WHOSE NAME WAS JUMP FREE, IN HONOR OF A NEW LION'S CONSCIOUSNESS, WHICH WAS

MORE CONCERNED WITH THE CARE OF THE YOUNG, OR THE WEAKER LIONS, WHO FOR ONE REASON OR ANOTHER, NEVER LEARNED WHEN YOUNG, HOW TO JUMP HIGH, TO REACH THE BRANCHES, AND HOW TO AVOID HARASSMENT FROM THE HUMAN HUNTERS.

BECAUSE OF THESE HUNTERS MANY LIONS WERE ORPHANED AND ROVED THE MORE DESOLATE LANDS OF THE COUNTRY FREE, AND LEARNING ON THEIR OWN TO SURVIVE. FINALLY, THE EASTERN COAST LIONS ELECTED THEIR OWN KING, THE REXARD FRICTION, AND THE SCHOLARLY COMMUNITY AT ZAIREKELY WAS DISBANDED, AND DISPERSED THROUGHOUT THE COUNTRY, LIKE THE ROAMING ORPHAN YOUTH. THE EASTERN COAST SUPPORTERS KING FRIXION STRUCK DEALS WITH THE HUMAN HUNTERS, THEY ARE THE ORPHANED YOUTH AND THE NOW ROAMING ZAIREKELIEN LIONS. THIS THEY DID TO GAIN NEW LANDS, AND TO CONTINUE THEIR FIGHT WITH THE TIGER FAMILIES IN MORE EASTERN LANDS LIKE VIET LAMB AND INDIA.

YOU SEE, IT IS THE ANIMAL NATURE, ONCE IN CONTACT WITH HUMANS, TO NEVER GET ENOUGH OF PROSPERITY AND FREEDOM. SO IT WAS THAT FATHER LION WAS TO ROAM THE INNER AFRICAN CONTINENT IN HIS YOUTH, AVOIDING THE HUMANS, AND THE TREACHERY OF THE EASTERN COMMUNITIES. DURING THIS TIME, HE 'DISCOVERED THE WONDERFULLY GENTLE NATURE OF MAMA LION, WHO BECAME THE RUNNING MATE, CONSTANT COMPANION, AND CONFIDANT.

DURING THIS TIME OF GREAT HARDSHIP AND DISUNITY AMONG THE LION FAMILY FATHER LION WAS REASSURED BY AN APHORISM OF THE GREAT GRANDFATHER LION, QUOTED BY HIS CLOSEST FRIEND, AND UNIVERSITY CLASSMATE, THE HONORABLE STEPHAN LION: "LIFE'S PLAY IS NOT MONSTROUS, JUST TRY TO PLAY MORE SOULFULLY, AND MORE DEVOTEDLY".

"A MYSTIC SENSATION CLUNG TO THE DUSKY AIR, AS THE TWO MEN SLOWLY PLOTTED THEIR

ROUTINE. CHEERFULLY BEARS PLAYED WITH THEIR CUBS, AND TINY SPIDER MONKEYS LEAPED FROM TREE TO CAGE. CHILDREN HAPPILY THRONGED THE WALKS, THROWING PEANUTS TO THE GIGANTIC AFRICAN ELEPHANTS, AND THE MEN WHO HAD BEEN WATCHING, PLANNING SOMETHING, BEGAN TO WHISPER, POINT, AND LINGER TOWARD THE LIONS' DEN.

UNLIKE THE WILDNESS THAT OFTEN ENTERS ANIMALS' HOMES WHEN LOOKED UPON BY STRANGERS, OR BY THEIR KEEPER, DON'T SUBTLE AND WARM FEELINGS OF TRUST FELL UPON THEIR HUMBLE FACES THIS EVENING. WHAT WOULD THIS NEW SCENT BRING, THOUGHT THE LIONS AND TIGERS, NOT CONTENT THIS EVENING TO LAY ABOUT THEIR CAGE?"

"THEY CAN SENSE IT," DAMIAN MUTTERED.

MONKEY WITH A BABY AND ELEPHANT

"THEN THEY WILL DO," HIS NEW FRIEND, BARNUM, REPLIED, WIPING THE SWEAT FROM HIS BROW.

THE TWO MEN SLIGHTLY GRINNED AND LOOKED DIRECTLY TOWARD THE HORIZON, AND ONCE AGAIN FELT NATURE'S WHISPERING WIND. THEY APPROACHED THE ZOO KEEPER'S DOOR AND KNOCKED: "MY, THAT TELEVISION'S LOUD! EXLAIMED MR. BARNUM.

"WHAT'S A 'TERRAVISION MAMA"? SAID EMMY, BACK IN THE DEN.

"IT'S WHAT HUMANS KEEP TIME WITH, EMMY. DON LIKES TO WATCH IT WHEN HE EATS, SO HE KNOWS WHAT TIME IT IS," MAMA LION AVERRED TO HER YOUNGEST.

"HMM, THE COSMETIC NEWSCAST, AND 8, 11 AND 12, LET'S NOT BE LATE, DAME. (P. T. BARNUM ALWAYS CALLED PEOPLE BY THE SYLLABLES OF THEIR NAMES,).

"SOUNDS LIKE DOGS BARKING," DAMIAN RESPONDED SLOWLY.

"I'M GOING OVER TO THEIR HOME. DAMIAN WALKED AWAY.

"HE'S A TRIANGLE OF THREE OPPOSITES: CURIOSITY, COMPETITIVENESS, AND RESTLESSNESS. HE IS ATTEMPTING TO BALANCE THEM IN A SOCIETY OF CONVENTION", DAMIAN PRIVATELY OBSERVED THE CIRCUS OWNER.

THEIR FOCUS AND THEIR MOTION STOPPED. THESE ONCE FEARLESS CREATURES MOMENTARILY QUIVERED AT THE SIGHT OF THE MAN IN THE DISTANCE, CARRYING SEVERAL BUCKETS OF FOOD.

THEIR APPREHENSION WAS NOT UNCALLED FOR AS THIS PARTICULAR ZOOKEEPER, DON, WAS A CRUEL AND HEARTLESS CARETAKER, QUITE ABLE TO HIDE HIS TRUE NATURE BEFORE THE HUMANS. HOWEVER, THIS VISIT WAS

DIFFERENT, BECAUSE ALONG WITH HIM WAS A STRANGE MAN.

AS THEY GOT CLOSER DON NOTICED THERE WAS A YOUNG MAN PETTING THE LIONS INSIDE THE CAGE.

"WHO DO YOU THINK YOU ARE, MESSING WITH MY LIONS BABE? HE SAID PASSIVELY, A VEIL OVER HIS HOSTILITY.

"MY NAME IS DAMIAN, AND I AM JUST GETTING ACQUAINTED WITH THESE MAGNIFICENT CREATURES."

"OH, THIS IS DAMIAN SANDERS, MY LION TAMER. HE'S FROM THE PYRENEES MOUNTAINS, HE IS A BASQUE," INTERJECTED MR. BARNUM, SOMEWHAT NERVOUSLY.

"A GYPSY, EH?" REMARKED DON WITH DETACHMENT. (—"LOSE YOUR BOTTLE, GENIE?" -DON THOUGHT TO HIMSELF, NOTING DAMIAN'S UNUSUAL OUTFIT.)

DAMIAN TURNED INVISIBLY, SLIPPING HIS HUNDRED SEVENTY-FIVE POUND BODY THROUGH THE CAGE BARS, AS QUICKLY AS THOUGHT ITSELF.

"AND, HOW DID YOU GET IN- HOW DID YOU DO THAT!?" DON CHALLENGED VEXATIOUSLY, OBSERVING HIM COME OUT OF THE CAGE BEFORE HIS QUESTION FINISHED.

"BY JOINING ALL THOUGHT WAVES SO THEY BECOME ONE WAVE ON THE GROSS AND SUBTLE FORMS OF THE ELEMENTS, ON THEIR ESSENTIAL CHARACTERISTICS AND THE INHERENCE OF THE GUNAS IN THEM, AND THE EXPERIENCES THEY PROVIDE FOR THE INDIVIDUAL, ONE GAINS MASTERY OF THE ELEMENTS DAMIAN QUIETLY ANSWERED.

"YOU'RE AN ILLUSIONIST, TOO, HUH?" ANOTHER CHALLENGE.

"THEN ALL THE ELEMENTS CEASE TO OBSTRUCT ONE," DON NOTICED HE GLOWED

MOMENTARITY, AND DISMISSED THE THOUGHT.

"SO, THESE ARE THE PRIDE?" ASKED BARNUM, CASTING A GLANCE AT THE THREE OR FOUR YOUNG LIONS CLOSING IN ON THE FRONT OF THE CAGE, WHO INCLUDED TANNY, EMMY, VINCENT, AND TACO, CAREFULLY LISTENING TO EVERY THOUGHT.

"ALL EXCEPT FOR THE BIG ONE, THEIR FATHER", HE POINTED TO THE YOUNG MALE AND FEMALE STANDING TOGETHER.

"WAY IN THE BACK THERE, SITTING STILL", DON SAID WITH DISTRACTION.

"WE'LL KEEP THEIR FATHER, HE FINISHED WITH THE AUTHORITY OF POWER. "IT DOESN'T SEEM RIGHT THAT TWO YOUNG LIONS SO NOBLE SHOULD BE SEPARATED FROM THE MALE PARENT. THEY WON'T DEVELOP AS I WISH THEM TO. HOW IS THEIR FATHER?" ASKED DAMIAN.

"HE GAZES A LOT ON THE SUNLIGHT, THOUGH HE'S IN EXCELLENT PHYSICAL CONDITION, ROARS LOUDEST IN THIS PRIDE, AND UNFORTUNATELY, I THINK THE SUN HAS CONE TO HIS HEAD. I'D LIKE TO SEE HIM TAKEN BACK TO THE DARK SIDE OF THE COMPLEX FOR 'LIGHT DEPRIVATION TRAINING THE TRUSTEES LIKE HIM, THOUGH, AND WON'T LET ME FOR NOW.

I'M WORKING ON IT, "HE YUKKED".

"IF YOU BUY THIS PRIDE, I'LL HAVE MY TREATMENT.

"I UNDERSTAND", GENTLED DAMIAN. OBSERVING THIS, BARNUM COULD SENSE THEM COULD ALMOST SEE THE CUBS TREMBLING: "WELL, WHATEVER, I WANT THEM ALL", SAID BARNUM. LITTLE EMMY AND VINCENT WERE STANDING NEXT TO ONE ANOTHER: EMMY SAID, "I WANT TO GO TO THE CIRCUS. HE CAN TALK TO US... HE CA-AN...

"I KNOW, SAID VINCENT, PEERING INTO DAMIAN'S WIDE-SET EYES OF HAZEL COLOR. WITH NO IMMEDIATE RESPONSE FROM THE ZOOKEEPER, BARNUM FELT OFFENDED AND THOUGHT:

"HOW COULD ANYONE NOT WANT THESE CREATURES IN THE WORLD-FAMOUS CIRCUS!?"

"LOTS OF BUCKS, HERE," THOUGHT THE KEEPER.

"WHAT ARE THESE SOULS TALKING ABOUT? "I THOUGHT THE LION TAMER."

"I'M SEEKING A VERY SPECIAL TIGER," SAID DAMIAN, WHO HAD SOUGHT FOR NEARLY THIRTY YEARS, SINCE HIS YOUTH.

"WELL, THERE YOU GO, DON WAVED HIS ARM IN FRONT OF DAMIAN'S FACE AND POINTED TO THE TIGER PRIDE TO THE LEFT. SAID DAMIAN, SHE'S NOT THERE."

"I'VE DECIDED, YOU DO WHAT YOU WANT WITH THE FATHER LION, WE'LL MEET TOMORROW AT ELEVEN WITH THE ATTORNEY, COMMANDED BARNUM. "I'LL HAVE THE CONTRACTS READY FOR SIGNATURE. ON THEIR RETURN TO THE HOTEL, DAMIAN ASKED P. T. TO TURN BACK. WHAT ARE WE DOING?" ASKED BARNUM.

"TURN AROUND," DAMIAN SAID IN A MONOTONE VOICE. HESITANTLY, BARNUM TURNED THE CAR AROUND. NOT KNOWING WHAT THEY WERE LOOKING FOR, WHAT THEY WERE DOING, THEY ENTERED THE GATE.

DAMIAN IMMEDIATELY WENT TO THE MAN IN CHARGE OF THE ZOO.

"DO YOU HAVE ANY MORE TIGERS?" ASKED DAMIAN IN A DETERMINED VOICE.

DON SAID, UNINTERESTED.

"YOU DON'T UNDERSTAND, I NEED TO SEE SOME MORE TIGERS!

DAMIEN, THE LION TAMER

MONKEY AT PLAY

DAMIAN STEPPED OUT OF HIS NORMAL COOL, BARNUM WAS SHOCKED, WITH HIS CURIOSITY GROWING ALONG WITH HIS IMPLICIT TRUST OF THIS TALL, LEAN GYPSY.

THE ZOOKEEPER LOOKED UP. "WHY DO YOU WANT TO SEE THE OTHER TIGERS?"

"YOU HAVE ANOTHER."

"YES, WHY?"

"LET ME SEE HER!"

THE THREE MEN WALKED THROUGH A GATE UNOPEN TO THE PUBLIC, AND INTO A DARK HUMID AREA. THEY OPENED THE DOOR TO A CAGE AND SAW A SICK, FEEBLE FEMALE TIGER.

DAMIAN JUST SMILED.

THE TRAINING

I KNOW THAT WHATSOEVER GOD DOETH IT SHALL BE FOREVER: NOTHING CAN BE PUT TO IT, NOR ANYTHING TAKEN FROM IT: AND GOD DOETH IT, THAT MEN SHOULD FEAR BEFORE HIM. THAT WHICH HAVE BEEN IS NOW, AND THAT WHICH IS TO BE HATH ALREADY BEEN; AND GOD REQUIRES THAT WHICH IS PAST. MOREOVER, I SAW UNDER THE SUN THE PLACE OF JUDGMENT, THAT WICKEDNESS WAS THERE; AND THE PLACE OF RIGHTEOUSNESS, THAT INIQUITY WAS THERE.

SAID IN MINE HEART, GOD SHALL JUDGE THE RIGHTEOUS AND THE WICKED: FOR THERE IS A TIME FOR EVERY PURPOSE AND EVERY WORK.

I SAID IN MY HEART CONCERNING THE SONS OF MEN, THAT GOD MIGHT MANIFEST THEM, AND THAT THEY MIGHT SEE THAT THEY ARE BEASTS. FOR THAT WHICH BEFALL THE SONS OF MEN BEFALL THE BEASTS; EVEN ONE THING FALLS THEM: AS THE ONE DIETH, SO DIETH THE

OTHER; YEA, THEY HAVE ALL ONE BREATH; SO THAT A MAN HATH NO PREEMINENCE ABOVE A BEAST: FOR ALL IS VANITY. ALL GO UNTO ONE PLACE; ALL ARE OF DUST, AND ALL TURN TO DUST AGAIN. WHO KNOWS THE SPIRIT OF MAN THAT GO UPWARD, AND THE SPIRIT OF THE BEAST THAT GOES DOWNWARD TO THE EARTH? WHEREFORE I PERCEIVE THAT THERE IS NOTHING BETTER THAN THAT A MAN SHOULD REJOICE IN HIS WORKS; FOR THAT IS HIS PORTION: FOR WHO SHALL BRING HIM TO SEE WHAT SHALL BE AFTER HIM?

SO, I RETURNED AND CONSIDERED ALL THE OPPRESSIONS THAT ARE DONE UNDER THE SUN: AND BEHOLD THE TEARS OF SUCH AS WERE OPPRESSED, AND THEY HAD NO COMFORTER, AND ON THE SIDE OF THEIR OPPRESSORS THERE WAS POWER, BUT THEY HAD NO COMFORTER. WHEREFORE I PRAISED THE DEAD WHICH ALREADY IS DEAD MORE THAN THE LIVING WHICH IS YET ALIVE. YEA, BETTER IS HE THAN BOTH THEY, WHICH HATH NOT BEEN, WHO HATH NOT SEEN THE EVIL

WORK THAT IS DONE UNDER THE SUN. AGAIN, I CONSIDERED ALL THE TRAVAIL, AND EVERY RIGHT WORK, THAT FOR THIS A MAN IS ENVIED OF HIS NEIGHBOR. THIS IS ALSO VANITY AND VEXATION OF SPIRIT. THE FOOL FOLDED HIS HANDS TOGETHER, AND EAT HIS FLESH. BETTER IS A HANDFUL WITH QUIETNESS, THAN BOTH HANDS FULL WITH TRAVAIL AND VEXATION OF SPIRIT.

THEN I RETURNED, AND I SAW VANITY UNDER THE SUN. - ECCLESIASTES 3 AND 4 THE CHAIRMAN OF THE BOARD OF TRUSTEES FOR THE STATE ZOO AT TIMESVILLE SIGNED THE DOCUMENT GRANTING TO P. T. BARNUM.

THE TWO PRIDES OF LIONS AND TIGERS, FOR THE SUM OF THREE MILLION, EIGHT HUNDRED AND FIFTY THOUSAND DOLLARS, IN U.S. CURRENCY AND GOLD. THE CONTRACT PROVIDED THAT FATHER LION BE LEFT BEHIND TO LEAD AND TRAIN THE NEW CAPTURES FROM THE AFRICAN AND ASIAN CONTINENTS, PLANNED BY THE GOVERNMENT, WITHIN THE

NEXT TWO YEARS THE ZOOKEEPER, DON, HAD CONVINCED THE TRUSTEES THAT FATHER LION WAS THE BEST ROLE MODEL FOR THE CONDITIONING THAT DON HAD ESTABLISHED AT THEIR ZOO, TO MAINTAIN ORDER. HE FURTHER PERSUADED THEM THAT BY THE TIME NEWCOMERS ARRIVED HE WOULD HAVE FATHER LION WAS SO PERFECTLY DISCIPLINED, THEY WOULD SIMPLY FOLLOW HIS EVERY EXAMPLE.

ALSO, DON RECOMMENDED, FATHER LION WOULD BE A GOOD SOLO EXHIBIT, SINCE HE WAS FIT, AND COULD SURVIVE ALONE, AND THAT HIS NEEDS COULD BE SATISFIED BY THE PUBLIC VISITING THE ZOO.

HIS CUBS, TANNY, VINCENT, EMMY, AND HIS MATE, MAMA LION, WOULD FIND ANOTHER SUITABLE FATHER, FROM OTHER P. T. BARNUM FINDS.

THE TRUSTEES AGREED TO DON'S PLAN TO PUT THE FATHER LION IN LIGHT, AIR, AND FOOD

DEPRIVATION TRAINING FOUR OUT OF EVERY SEVEN DAYS OF THE WEEK, TO ACCOMPLISH WHAT DON TOLD THEM WERE THE LATEST IN ANIMAL TRAINING DEVICES, AND GOALS, FOR ANIMAL HEALTH, AND ANIMAL CARE.

EARLIER THAT DAY, JUST BEFORE SUNRISE THE GREEN GLINT OF DAWN AND A FEW MILD ROARS AWOKE VINCENT, WHO WAS ALSO CALLED VINCENT ALLAN LION:

"THEY ONLY ROAR AFTER THEY'VE SLEPT TOGETHER"

"HUMM, WHAT, VINCENT?" AWOKE TANNY.

THE GROWN VINCENT. - "THEY ONLY ROAR AFTER THEY'VE SLEPT TOGETHER, AND MADE LOVE, DURING THE NIGHT, OR IN THE MORNING"

"HOW DO YOU KNOW THAT?"

"HAVEN'T YOU NOTICED?" "YEAH, I GUESS SO.

"I DON'T WANNA' GROW UP IF THAT'S THE ONLY TIME I CAN ROAR MY ROAR," CLAIMED EMMY, LYING ON HER SIDE AWAY FROM HER BROTHERS.

EMMY! "YOU'RE AWAKE!? I THOUGHT YOU WERE SLEEPING LIKE A SKY. SAID VINCENT.

"I WANT TO ROAR ALL DAY! SHE JUMPED UP AND STRETCHED, PULLING IN HER STOMACH, AND RAISING THE SMALL OF HER BACK:

"REAR," SHE GAVE OUT, WITH A HEAD MOTION.

TANNY LAUGHED WITH JOY, AS DID VINCENT. THE SUN WAS NOW CREATING A GOLDEN GLOW ON THE PRIDE.

CRACK...DRANG, THE GLOW WAS FLASHED BY DON'S STRIKING THE CAGE WITH HIS CHAIN:

I'LL BET YOUR NEW GOLDEN BOY MASTER COULDN'T SLIP THROUGH THE BARS WITH THESE ON HIM, HE LAUGHED BAUDILY.

"IN MY HAND HERE I HOLD THE HIGHEST POWER KNOWN TO MAN ON THIS EARTH'. "HE WHIPPED THE CHAIN AGAIN, MISSING ALL BUT THE BOTTOM OF THE BARS, AND CONCRETE, WHEN HE TURNED HIS RIGHT FOOT OUTWARDS, AND AT THE SAME TIME BURPED A TASTE OF FRIED EGG AND SAUSAGE, FROM THE MC DONALDS ON THE OUTSKIRTS OF TIMESVILLE.

LOOKING AT VINCENT ALLAN TO REASSURE HIMSELF, HE SAID: "YOUR DADDY'S GOT SOME SURPRISES IN STORE FOR HIM, BABE. I KNOW A LITTLE ABOUT THE LAW AND A LITTLE ABOUT THE LAWS OF NATURE

THINKING THE LIONS AND TIGERS COULD NOT COMPREHEND HIS INTENT, HE BEGAN TO THROW IN THE FATTY FLANKS, MORE RECENTLY DEVOID OF LEAN MEAT, SINCE HE AND A LOCAL CORPORATION ENTERED AN AGREEMENT HE AND A FRIEND HAD DEVISED.

(DON HAD BEEN A MESS COOK WITH THE U.S. AIR FORCE, BEFORE MAKING HIS WAY UP TO THE KEEPER POSITION HERE, AND WAS FAIRLY FAMILIAR WITH RULES OF FOOD AND SERVICE BARTERING THAT OUTSIDERS NEVER SPOKE OF).

"WHAT'S HE TALKING ABOUT, FATHER'S GONNA' BE PUT IN A STORE WITH SURPRISES?" REACTED LITTLE EMMY TO VINCENT ALLAN LION.

"I'M NOT SURE, EMMY I WONDER IF FATHER KNOWS, AND I DON'T THINK IT'S GOOD

VINCENT QUIETLY SLIPPED FROM SIGHT. FATHER LION PUT FIRST THINGS FIRST IN HIS LIFE, AND ALWAYS AROSE BEFORE DAWN EACH DAY FOR HIS LION'S MEDITATION, TO DETERMINE THE ELEMENTS, AND REGENERATE A LION'S COURAGE, AN ACT, WHICH FOR LIONS, DOES NOT COME INSTINCTIVELY, AS HUMANS BELIEVE, BUT WHICH IS REIGNITED LIKE A COAL STOVE IS RE-FIRED EACH MORNING IN WINTER.

"YES, I KNOW," HE SAID TO VINCENT, "MY HEARTS FLAME ROSE POWERFULLY BRIGHT THIS DAY, LIGHTING A VISION OF A TERRIBLE FUTURE HARDSHIP FOR ME, AND MY FAMILY, HE IS NEAR IS RE-FIRED

HE IN NEAR SILENCE, GAVE RESPONSE TO VINCENT'S APPROACH WITHOUT A WORD.

VINCENT UNDERSTOOD THAT WHICH IS MOST STRONG IS TAUGHT IN SILENCE, THAT WHICH LASTS, IS TAUGHT IN SILENCE. THIS MUCH HE LEARNED FROM FATHER LION.

"WHAT CAN WE DO, FATHER?"

"MAKE NO COMPROMISES WITH FEAR, VINCENT, SURRENDER COMPLETELY TO IT, AND FOLLOW WITH COMPLETE COMMITMENT THE DIRECTION OF THIS DAMIAN, THE LION TAMER. I HAVE NEVER CROSSED THE PATH OF ONE HUMAN SUCH AS HE, THOUGH THE SCRIPTURES LEFT THE GREAT-GRANDFATHER LION SAYS THAT THERE ARE HUMANS LIKE

HE, THAT HAVE THE LION'S COURAGE AND STRENGTH, AND WHO LOVES US, AS ONE OF HIS OWN."

"HOW DID YOU KNOW THIS? WERE' NT YOU IN EVENING MEDITATION WHEN HE CAME INTO THE CAGE?"

"YES, SON, I WAS. WHAT I FELT AND SAW, NO ONE ELSE SAW: LIGHT SHOT FROM HIS FINGERTIPS TOWARD ME AND INTO ME AS THOUGH HE KNEW ME WELL AND KNEW WHAT IS TO BE DONE TO ME. I SAW HIS LIGHT, AND T UNDERSTOOD HIS HIGH SPIRIT. I RAISED PAW IN THANKS.

"NOW, BRING MAMA LION, TANNY, AND EMMY HERE TO ME." "YES, FATHER" VINCENT HURRIED.

DON AND HIS ASSISTANT WERE PULLING OUT THE HIGH-PRESSURE HOSES TO CLEAN THE CAGES OF THE PRIDE FIRST, SO THEY WOULD BE DRY WHEN BARNUM'S PEOPLE ARRIVED TO REMOVE THEM.

THE LION TAMER

P. T. BARNUM, A CONSCIENTIOUS BUSINESSMAN, WAKENED HIMSELF EVERY MORNING AT FIVE-THIRTY AND BEGAN WORK ON HIS GAME PLAN. ARRIVING NEARLY TWO AND A HALF HOURS EARLY TO THE ZOO BEFORE HIS ATTORNEY, WAS PART OF THAT GAME PLAN.

A MAN WITH AN ASTUTE UNDERSTANDING OF MEN AND ANIMALS, HE WAS NOT SURPRISED TO SEE DON PERFUNCTORILY HOSTING MEMBERS OF THE PRIDE, IN A KIND OF TARGET PRACTICE, ALONG WITH THEIR SURROUNDINGS FOR A BRIEF PERIOD, HE OBSERVED SECRETLY THE BODY LANGUAGE OF THIS KEEPER AND FINALLY APPROACHED WITH A CHEERFUL GOOD MORNING.

"GOO-OOD MORNING MR. BARNUM, TOP O THE MORNING TO YOU," SAID DON, WITHOUT EYE CONTACT.

"WHERE'S YOUR LION TAMER THIS MORNING? PERFORMING MAGIC TRICKS FOR THE

CHILDREN AT THE SCHOOLS?" - HE LAUGHED REASSURINGLY THAT HE MEANT NO DISRESPECT.

"SAY, MR. BARNUM, SIR, HOW IN THE HECK DID HE SQUEEZE THROUGH THOSE BARS THE WAY HE DID YESTERDAY?"

"I DON'T KNOW, DON, HE MUST BE WORKING FROM SOME HIGHER POWER THAN WE ARE THAT MUCH I'M SURE OF.

"ANYTHING'S POSSIBLE, HA HA." HE COUGHED SEVERAL TIMES, UNTIL REGAINING CONTROL OF A CHOKE.

FATHER LION ASKED THE FAMILY AROUND HIM, DESPITE OCCASIONAL DRIPS OF HEAVY WATER SPRAY ON MAMA LION'S LONG MAIN.

"I WILL NEED YOU EACH TO MEDITATE FOR ME, DURING MY TIME HERE ALONE, AS I BELIEVE MY MEDITATIONS ALONE MAY NOT BE POWERFUL ENOUGH. I HAVE TAUGHT YOU THE DISCIPLINE,

THE. TIME, BEFORE YOU START YOUR DAY, AND THE PRACTICE

"NOW WAIT A MINUTE," JOHN LION, MAMA LION INTERRUPTED IN FRUSTRATION, AS ANOTHER FLOCK OF HARD WATER CAUGHT HER HIND QUARTER, AND A GIDDY LAUGH FROM DON, WITH A COMMENT ABOUT KNOWING JUST WHERE TO PUT IT, "THESE KIDS ARE GOING TO HAVE A HARD-ENOUGH TIME, WITHOUT HAVING SOME SPIRITUAL REGIMEN, AND MORE DISCIPLINE PUT ON THEM. YOU CAN SHOW THEM THIS STUFF WHEN THEY'RE GROWN, IT DOESN'T MAKE SENSE TO ADD TO THEIR BURDEN."

ALL WERE FEELING FRUSTRATED AT THIS MOMENT, AND EACH WAS FAIRLY WELL WET. MAMA LION WAS PUTTING UP A LINE OF DEFENSE ALL KNEW WAS AGAINST A HEAVIER BURDEN, AND THEY SAID NOTHING. IT WAS THE LOSS OF HIM, THE YEARS OF STRUGGLE TOGETHER, BEFORE THE CUBS ENTERED THEIR LIVES, BEFORE AND AFTER THEIR CAPTURE

TOGETHER BY THE RUDE HUMAN GROUPS THEY SUFFERED THROUGH COURAGEOUSLY, AND THROUGH THE FRUSTRATIONS TO THEIR GROWTHS, IN THE MANY ZOOS, BEFORE TIMESVILLE.

FATHER LION PUT HIS STRONG JAW AGAINST HER NECK, AS ALL LION MATES DO, AND SAID TO ALL: "NOW NO MORE TALK, THIS DAY HAS SPECIAL MAGIC, AS YOU WILL SOON MEET A HUMAN MASTER WITH COMPASSION AND GREAT LIGHT. THIS DAY, DESPITE, WILL BE SWEET, AND EVEN I WILL TAKE JOY IN KNOWING YOU ARE ALL WELL CARED FOR. I PROMISE WE'LL BE REUNITED AGAIN; I SENSE IT IN MY LION'S EYE. PLEASE THINK OF ME ALWAYS WITH PURITY, AS I KNOW YOU WILL, AND I WILL SURVIVE."

THE LITTLE FAMILY HUGGED AND CARESSED EACH OTHER FOR A TIME, AND MAMA LION CLUTCHED AT FATHER LION'S GREAT SHOULDER, WITH HER JAW TIGHTLY AGONIZED AGAINST HER CHEST, AND HER HEAD DOWN.

"HUMANS DON'T SEE THE NOW IN EVERY MOMENT," SAID OTHELLO, A BIG, PREDOMINANTLY BLACK BENGAL OF MIDDLE AGE.

"SO, WHAT DO THEY WANT WITH US?" HE ASKED HIS MATE, BINDU BENGAL HER FACE RELAXED, AND SILENTLY SHE MOVED HER CHIN SLIGHTLY UPWARDS, AS BENGAL FEMALES DO TO INDICATE THAT THERE MAY NOT BE AN ANSWER TO THIS QUESTION.

THE BENGAL IS SIMPLE, ALTHOUGH THE HUMANS SAY, FEROCIOUS. IN INDIA, THERE IS MUCH CONFUSION OVER THE BEHAVIOR AND THE MOTIVES OF THE BENGAL TIGERS. MEN STUDY THEM, TO TRAP THEM, AND EVERY YEAR SOME OF THE GREATEST VETERAN BENGAL MEDITATORS ARE TAKEN APART BY THE CREATURE, AS THOUGH A SACRIFICE TO SOME TIGER GOD, WHO COMES OUT IN THE MOONLIGHT, OR AT DAWN, TO GIVE PERMISSION TO THE TIGER, TO MAKE HIS OR HER MOVE.

"OUR COUSINS, THE PUMA TIGER, AND THE COUGAR TIGER (MOUNTAIN LION) WERE REVERED BY THE RED HUMANS IN THIS LAND, AND LEFT ALONE, UNTIL THE WHITE HUMANS CAME WITH FIRE STICKS TO CHASE THEM NORTH, AND NORTH AGAIN. OTHELLO CONTINUED IN CONTEMPLATION:

"THE COUGAR-PUMA GOD MUST BE WORSHIPPED VERY STRONGLY I HAVE NEVER HEARD OF THEM IN HUMAN ZOOS."

"DAMIAN IS COMING", SAID BINDU.

"YES, I SENSE HIS PRESENCE, REPLIED OTHELLO, HE IS A HUMAN WHO KNOWS THE NOW."

"I FEEL WE CAN TRUST HIM," SAID BINDU

"WHICH IS THE SUPERIOR CREATURE, DAME, THE BENGAL, OR THE LION?" ASKED P. T.

"THEY ARE BOTH SIMPLE," REPLIED DAMIAN.

"THE TIGER SEEMS SO MYSTERIOUS I SO CALCULATING ADDED MR. BARNUM.

IS SIMPLE," REITERATED DAMIAN.

"YOU NEED US ARTISTS WE CALM YOU DOWN, COOL OFF THE DRIVES THAT GETS HOPELESS."

A LITTLE OFF GUARD, YET SMILING, BARNUM REPLIED: "YOU'RE RIGHT AS USUAL DAME. THEY ARE BEAUTIFUL, TAKE GOOD CARE TIL I COME BACK FROM NEW YORK." DAMIAN OFFERED HIM HIS HAND.

DAMIAN ENTERED THE TIMESVILLE BIG TOP, THE HUGE TENT OF THE P. T. BARNUM TRAVELING CIRCUS. WALKING ACROSS THE FLOOR OF SAWDUST LAID YESTERDAY, HE APPROACHED THE DOME CAGE OF STEEL WELDED WITH PRECISION BY PIPE FITTERS, WITH ITS STEELY SPINES REACHING UPWARD TO A POINT AT THE CENTER. THREE TIMES THE SIZE OF THEIR CAGE AT THE ZOO, BOTH PRIDES WAITED EAGERLY FOR THE RETURN OF DAMIAN.

INDEED, TIME WOULD NOT WAIT FOR THE SORCERY OF DAMIAN. WITH HIS GOLDEN HAIR AND HAZEL EYES, YOU WOULD NEVER GUESS HE WAS SO STRONG AND ABLE TO HANDLE SUCH CREATURES— -—THE LIONS AND THE TIGERS.

DAMIAN'S INAUGURAL ADDRESS TO THE PRIDE "YOU CAME FROM THE WORLD, AND NOW YOU LIVE IN A SOCIETY THAT IS NOT HAPPY UNLESS IT IS EITHER GELDING, OR REMOVING THE DIGNITY FROM, SOMETHING, OR SOMEONE THAT SEES ALL BEINGS OTHER THAN ITS LIKE, AS PROPERTY AND THAT TREATS ITS OWN THE SAME, AS A RESULT. THE MONKEY HAS A TREE, AND THE WOLF HAS A HOLE.

MAN, CALLS THESE THEIR TERRITORIES. MAN CLAIMS EVERY BEING IDENTICAL TO HIMSELF, YET AT THE SAME TIME, SOMEHOW INFERIOR TO HIM IN KNOWLEDGE. MAN IS BESTIAL IN EVERY MOVEMENT, AND IN HIS PRIVATE LIFE YET CALLS HIMSELF THE MOST DIVINELY LINKED OF ALL BEINGS ON THIS PLANET.

LIKE MR. BARNUM, YOUR OWNER, IS CURIOUS, RESTLESS, AND COMPETITIVE. HE WAGES WAR ON THOSE IN PAIN, IN NAMES LIKE THE WAR ON DRUGS, AND WAR ON THE POOR, IN THE NAME OF THE WAR ON POVERTY. HE OWNS THE DOUBT AND SKEPTICISM OF THE HUMAN LAWYER, HE IS SCATTERED IN HIS CONCENTRATION, AND IN THIS LAND, HE EXPORTS THE VIOLENCE HE FEELS FROM OUTSIDE PRESSURES, DESTROYING THE LIFE OF OTHER HUMANS ORGANIZED DIFFERENTLY THAN HE IS ORGANIZED.

YOUR COUSIN, THE BABY CALF, HE EATS, BEFORE IT HAS GROWN. TO MAKE ITS FLESH EASIER TO CHEW, HE BREAKS THE BABY'S LEGS AND KEEPS IT IN A BOX THE SIZE OF ITS SMALL BODY. SINCE THE CHILD CAN NOT MOVE IT GROWS FATTY AND TENDER AND ITS LIFE IS TAKEN BEFORE IT SEES ADULTHOOD. THE CALF'S PARENTS, THE BULL AND COW, ARE ALSO EATEN, AND WITH NEEDLES ARE INJECTED WITH 27,000 DIFFERENT FLUIDS,

TO MAKE THEM MORE CHEWABLE BY THE HUMANS.

SOME HUMANS REFUSE TO TAKE PART IN THE TAKING OF LIFE THIS WAY, AND THEY ARE USUALLY ASKED TO RETURN TO 'THE RIGHT PATH' AGAIN, FOR THE SAKE OF THEIR 'HEALTH' DESPITE THE GREAT STRENGTH OF THEIR DECISION.

DAMIAN PAUSED. EVERY EYE WAS UPON HIM, COMMUNICATING WITHOUT WORDS HIS ADDRESS:

"MAN HAS FIRST COMMANDMENT FOR HIS LIFE

'THOU SHALT NOT PLACE FALSE GODS BEFORE ME AND ANOTHER,

'THOU SHALT NOT KILL'. THESE, AND EIGHT OTHERS, INCLUDING

'THOU SHALT NOT COVET THE WIFE OF THY NEIGHBOR' THE HUMAN

LEADER, MOSES, IS SAID TO HAVE RECEIVED FROM THE MOUTH OF THE SUPREME GODHEAD, LONG BEFORE YOUR GREAT GRANDFATHER LION.

THE GREAT GRANDFATHER LION'S FIRST SON, THE GREAT LION OF JUDAH, SAID OF THESE COMMANDMENTS:

'AS TO THE LAWS OF MOSES, I HAVE ENDEAVORED TO ESTABLISH THEM IN THE HEARTS OF MEN. AND I SAY UNTO YOU THAT YOU DO NOT UNDERSTAND THEIR REAL MEANING, FOR IT IS NOT VENGEANCE HUT MERCY THAT THEY TEACH; ONLY THE SENSE OF THESE LAWS HAS BEEN PERVERTED. NEVERTHELESS, THERE IS ONE MIRACLE THAT A MAN CAN ACCOMPLISH. IT IS WHEN FULL OF A SINCERE BELIEF, HE DECIDES TO ROOT OUT FROM HIS HEART ALL EVIL THOUGHTS, AND WHEN TO ATTAIN HIS END HE FORSAKES THE PATHS OF INIQUITY. AND ALL THE THINGS THAT ARE DONE WITHOUT GOD ARE BUT ERRORS, SEDUCTIONS, AND ENCHANTMENTS, WHICH

ONLY DEMONSTRATE TO WHAT AN EXTENT THE SOUL OF HIM WHO PRACTICES THIS ART IS FULL OF SHAMELESSNESS, FALSEHOOD, AND IMPURITY.

"IT IS THESE" THEN, WHAT ABOUT FATHER LION!? "LITTLE EMMY CUB BLURTED OUT, AND THEN QUICKLY RESERVED HERSELF, WITH "MASTER, DAMIAN?"

"WELL, FROM THE MOUTHS OF BABES… WE KNOW, ALL OF US, WHAT IS BEING DONE TO FATHER LION, AND THERE WILL BE A PLAN, AND HE WILL BE FREED TO RETURN TO YOU, I PROMISE." SAID DAMIAN, BEAMING BOTH EYES ON EMMY, WITHOUT A BLINK.

"WE MUST BEGIN.," COMMANDED DAMIAN.

THE LONG AND FULL DAYS OF TRAINING PASSED QUICKLY WITH DAMIAN, STARTING WITH SHORT JUMPS FROM PEDESTALS TO PEDESTALS OF VARYING HEIGHTS, FROM PEDESTALS TO FLOOR, AND FLOOR TO PEDESTALS.

THE FIVE O'CLOCK CHURCH BELL RANG, AND THE YOUNGER LIONS WERE FAMISHED. THE BENGALS HONED AND HONED.

BY JON ALBERT BUCHNESS 1990

EMMY THE LION CUB

www.ingramcontent.com/pod-product-compliance
Lightning Source LLC
LaVergne TN
LVHW020415070526
838199LV00054B/3622